IMAGES
of America

SAN FRANCISCO'S
TREASURE ISLAND

This photograph shows Treasure Island as it appeared from February 1939 until September 1940, when the Golden Gate International Expo was in full swing. This view looks north across Treasure Island from Yerba Buena Island. The Tower of the Sun can be seen prominently on the left. In the Port of the Trade Winds in the center is a Sikorsky S-42 clipper. (Author's collection.)

ON THE COVER: This grand view looks south down the Court of the Seven Seas to the Tower of the Sun, prominent in the rear. This view is perhaps the most spectacular of the entire fair. (Author's collection.)

IMAGES
of America

SAN FRANCISCO'S
TREASURE ISLAND

Jason Pipes

ARCADIA
PUBLISHING

Published by Arcadia Publishing
Charleston SC, Chicago IL, Portsmouth NH, San Francisco CA

Printed in the United States of America

Library of Congress Catalog Card Number: 2006939750

For all general information contact Arcadia Publishing at:
Telephone 843-853-2070
Fax 843-853-0044
E-mail sales@arcadiapublishing.com
For customer service and orders:
Toll-Free 1-888-313-2665

Visit us on the Internet at www.arcadiapublishing.com

This book is dedicated to the men and women of the U.S. Armed Services, past and present, who put their lives in harm's way to protect the freedoms and liberties we so value.

Shown is an artist's impression of Treasure Island once the planned San Francisco Airport was completed. Although some of the details shown are correct, others are not. The main buildings on Treasure Island are present in their correct forms, but the parking facilities, causeway, and landing areas were overly idealized. As it was, the airport never came to the island; it wasn't practical, and the navy took control after 1940. (Author's collection.)

CONTENTS

ACKNOWLEDGMENTS

I would like to thank the countless number of people that have helped with the creation of this book. Foremost is my wonderful partner, Petra Esterle, for her countless hours spent helping find Treasure Island materials as well as for her expertise with photography and proofreading. In addition, her moral support helps me to achieve what I do each day. Thanks also goes to Todd Lappin for his like-minded quest to explore and document abandoned military bases and for the use of photographs from his personal archive; to Robert Glass of the National Archives in San Bruno for his assistance in locating and making sense of the Treasure Island archives; to Mark Wertheimer of the United States Naval Historical Center in Washington, D.C., for his invaluable assistance and direction regarding Naval Station Treasure Island; to John Poultney for believing in this book and helping to get it published; to the firefighters of San Francisco Fire Department Station 48; to Taylor Pipes for giving me the inspiration to get this book published and for being a great friend through good times and bad; to Travis Pipes for his verve and drive to succeed, which inspires me daily; to Martha Pipes for raising me through thick and thin; and to Robert Pipes for imbuing in me the inspiration to appreciate critical thinking and for giving me the passion to pursue historical research. A very special thank you to Bill Larkin, Ray Raineri, and John Harder for access to their extensive collections for use in this book. If there is someone I have forgotten to thank, I dearly apologize. This work would not have been possible without all of you.

INTRODUCTION

Treasure Island is a recent creation, geologically speaking, in the Bay Area. As recent, that is, as the vaunted Golden Gate and Bay Bridges, all being built in the mid-1930s. But 70 years have passed since construction began, and 70 years is a long time in human ages—not long at all in the gaze of the islands nearby, like Yerba Buena Island and Angel Island, but long enough for its history to have evolved through many phases and for memories of its past to have become murky and forgotten.

When Treasure Island was first constructed, it was viewed (rightfully) as an engineering marvel and technological masterpiece. It was hailed as the largest man-made island in the world, and although a few other locations in 1936 could contend that notion, it was largely true. When the Golden Gate International Exposition was held on Treasure Island in 1939 and 1940, there were not many who did not know its importance or notice its location. During World War II, the navy took control, and hundreds of thousands of men passed through the island, emphasizing its critical importance. Afterward Treasure Island was home to a vitally important navy base, which until 1997 was crucial in the defense of the Pacific region.

In 2007, ten years after the navy left Treasure Island, much less traffic populates the once-bustling base. Home now to about 2,000 residents and a handful of businesses, the island has settled into a relaxed period to which previously it had not been accustomed. This lull will not last much longer, as San Francisco will soon see Treasure Island transformed into an entirely different place. It will not be the product of military requirements or a world's fair but a much sought-after urban development. This development project will, in all likelihood, take into account housing for rich and poor, commercial and residential areas, parkland and open space, community activities, art, public transportation, and much more. Treasure Island has the potential to become, unlike almost any other space in the Bay Area, transformed entirely into a place as magical and important as it has been in the past.

The idea to construct a man-made island in the San Francisco Bay began in the early 1930s. Joseph Dixon is credited with suggesting that a world's fair be held in San Francisco in 1933, and many others shortly thereafter are credited with helping to come up with what was deemed an ideal location for not only a world's fair but a new municipal airport as well. San Francisco mayor Angelo Rossi, Gov. Frank Merriam, members of the chamber of commerce, the San Francisco City Council, and various business and political figures in California all helped spur forward a plan to construct Treasure Island. Perhaps no figure played as much of a role in Treasure Island's creation as Leland Cutler, for it was he whom the mayor appointed to work on funding the project. And fund it he did. After working in Washington, D.C., Cutler managed to secure $3.8 million from the Works Progress Administration (WPA) for the purpose of building a new San Francisco airport. This WPA-sponsored project would be the third largest in all of California, the others being the Golden Gate Bridge and the Bay Bridge. Together these three projects would literally transform San Francisco and the Bay Area into a modern, vibrant, and flourishing place firmly rooted in the modern era. With WPA funding secured, Cutler and the mayor finalized an additional $750,000 from San Francisco business leaders and civic groups to cap off the project. In the end, the final cost of Treasure Island and the expo held there would amount to $40 million.

The location chosen for Treasure Island was to the north of Yerba Buena Island in a spot known as the Yerba Buena Shoals. Yerba Buena Shoals was deemed an ideal location to build an entirely man-made island. Construction began on February 11, 1936, and was overseen by the U.S. Army Corps of Engineers. It took 18 months to finish the project, which was completed on August 24, 1937.

When construction of Treasure Island was complete, preparations for the World's Fair to be held in 1939 began in earnest and would continue for another 17 months. The World's Fair, to be known as the Golden Gate International Exposition of 1939, was slated to open on February 19, 1939. It would not be incorrect to suggest that the amount of work that went into the construction of the World's Fair on Treasure Island equaled that of the Yerba Buena Shoals fill project itself. Nearly 6,000 workers spent millions of hours erecting fair buildings and pavilions, landscaping the grounds, painting, setting up lighting, and providing highlights in the form of accents, art, and architectural flair.

When the World's Fair opened on Treasure Island in February 1939, the Bay Area and much of the West Coast watched closely. The success of the expo would have a great impact on dozens of civic and private ventures. In any case, the public would enjoy the fair regardless of its economic stimulus or the critical thought generated by its nuances. The expo would continue for nearly two years between February 19, 1939, and September 29, 1940. It was open nearly every day and greeted millions of visitors from around the world during its run. Tens of thousands of shows, presentations, bands, dance groups, special events, attractions, and exciting fair offerings were put on for the public during the expo. The number of things a person could do and see at the fair would require an enormous tome to detail but included everything from carnival rides and dare-devil shows to burlesque reviews, art shows, famous figures, movie stars, pop-culture icons, cultural ethnographies, culinary offerings, historical artifacts, and museum displays. There was literally something for everyone on Treasure Island during the fair. Expo presentations were housed in semi-permanent buildings akin to those built for the 1915 Panama-Pacific Exposition in San Francisco, of which the Palace of Fine Arts is the sole remainder (none remain from the expo on Treasure Island save for the three buildings built permanently at the southern end). Buildings were constructed of Douglas fir planking, coated in layers of stucco, and painted in an official range of expo-designed colors. The World's Fair ended on September 29, 1940, and had attracted 16 million visitors before it closed.

Shortly before the expo ended, Rear Adm. John Greenslade of the 12th Naval District, based in San Francisco, suggested to Washington, D.C., that the government acquire Treasure Island, but the idea was rejected. Not to be let down, Greenslade pressed the issue locally and managed to be granted its use under a declaration of national emergency with the looming threat of World War II. The understanding was that it would be given back when the crisis had passed. On February 28, 1941, Treasure Island was leased to the navy in exchange for land near Millbrae that San Francisco could use for its planned airport expansion instead of Treasure Island. Furious naval construction took place during this time, transforming the island into a vast patrol and security base, training facility, and receiving station. On April 1, 1941, the island officially became known as Naval Station Treasure Island. The navy was present on Treasure Island when Japan attacked Pearl Harbor on December 7, 1941. Dozens of private citizens turned out at Treasure Island to loan their watercraft to aid in patrolling the Golden Gate to protect it from the expected Japanese attack that thankfully never came. On April 17, 1942, the U.S. Navy formally seized Treasure Island from San Francisco with a "declaration of taking and deposit," allowing it to take sole and permanent ownership of the land.

During World War II, Treasure Island was used as a center for receiving, training, and dispatching service personnel. In this period, exposition structures were temporarily used for barracks and training centers. Notably the former Foods and Beverages Building was converted into the largest mess hall in the country, serving 7,000 meals an hour. This massive building would later burn to the ground in an inferno that engulfed it in April 1947.

After World War II ended in August 1945, Naval Station Treasure Island continued to serve as a valuable and permanent receiving center, training station, and naval homeport for thousands of naval personnel. Toward the end of the cold war, when the idea of a 600-ship navy was eventually set aside, Treasure Island was deemed no longer crucial to the defense of the United States. It was slated for closure by the Base Realignment and Closure Commission in 1995 along with many other Bay Area military institutions, to take effect in 1997. With the sound of bugles at sunset after speeches by navy commanders and Mayor Willie Brown, a ceremonial guard lowered the flag at Naval Station Treasure Island for the final time on May 8, 1997. San Francisco took formal control of the island on September 30, 1997, although the navy still controlled many of the buildings until the final closure and hand-over process was resolved.

In addition to WPA projects, a World's Fairs, and a military base, Treasure Island has also been home to numerous movies. A partial list of features that have included Treasure Island or that have been filmed on location include *Father's Day* (1997), *Indiana Jones and the Last Crusade* (1989), *Flubber* (1997), *What Dreams May Come* (1998), *Patch Adams* (1998), *Bicentennial Man* (1999), *Copy Cat* (1995), *The Matrix* (1999), *The Caine Mutiny* (1954), *Charlie Chan at Treasure Island* (1939), *Treasure Island* (2000), *Rent* (2005), *The Incredible Hulk* (2003), *Nash Bridges* (1996–2001), and *Battlebots* (2000–2002).

It is hoped that this work will spur new interest in the history of Treasure Island. Given the sheer volume of material available in print on historical topics related to Northern California and the San Francisco Bay area, it is amazing that no works are currently in print on Treasure Island. Of those that have been published, only five have been specifically about Treasure Island, and only one was widely available when it was in print. The following list is provided to help those wishing to further pursue this amazing subject and includes nearly all the works one should consult when first researching this topic. The list includes *The Art of Treasure Island* by Eugen Neuhaus; *Guardians of the Golden Gate* by Ralph Shanks; *High Steel: Building the Bridges across the San Francisco Bay* by Dillon, Thomas, and DeNevi; *Natural History of the Islands of California* by Schoenherr, Feldmeth, and Emerson; *The Naval History of Treasure Island*, edited by E. McDevitt; *Official Guide Book: Golden Gate International Exposition*; *San Francisco Bay* by Harold Gilliam; *San Francisco Bay: A Pictorial Maritime History* by John Kimble; *Treasure Island: The Magic City* by Jack Jones; *Treasure Island: San Francisco's Exposition Years* by Richard Reinhardt; and *Wings over the Orient* by Stan Cohen.

San Francisco mayor Angelo Rossi (seated) and his staff view the early details of the planned airport on Treasure Island. As events were to play out, the airport never came to Treasure Island, even though construction of Treasure Island was based on it being there. (Courtesy of Ray Raineri collection.)

This is another view of San Francisco mayor Angelo Rossi (left) and his staff viewing early details of the airport to be built on Treasure Island once the island was complete. This view clearly shows the public-relations nature of these images taken in the very early 1930s. (Courtesy of Ray Raineri collection.)

One

BUILDING

TREASURE ISLAND
1936–1939

The location chosen for Treasure Island was a shallow region north of Yerba Buena Island known as the Yerba Buena Shoals. The Yerba Buena Shoals were known for their shallow depths and nearly impassable bars and were an ideal location to construct a man-made island. In addition to their potential for rising above the surface of the bay, they also lay directly astride the path of the new Bay Bridge, allowing for easy automobile access.

Construction of Treasure Island began on February 11, 1936. Building the island was overseen by numerous agencies and headed by the U.S. Army Corps of Engineers as well as the WPA, the San Francisco Public Utilities Commission, and the Public Works Administration. Various dredges, barges, lifts, cranes, and diggers worked non-stop to complete the island. The construction process involved dredging, digging, dumping, and pouring 25 million cubic yards of material from all across the bay into an area one and a half miles long by one mile wide, all within a boulder retaining wall stretching around a three-mile-long perimeter. The very name of the island itself came from this process: "Treasure Island" is a reference to the presence of trace amounts of gold in the newly formed island. This was so because the fill for Treasure Island came directly from the same places the forty-niners had found gold 90 years before, albeit washed across 150 miles of Central Valley rivers before dumping into the San Francisco Bay.

Even before construction of the island was completed, three permanent buildings on the island were started—the administration building and two large airplane hangars. All three were located along the southern end, affording them the most stable and solid foundation. In addition to the fill for the island, workers were also responsible for building the causeway connecting Treasure Island to Yerba Buena Island and the ramps to connect the causeway to the Bay Bridge. The Yerba Buena Shoals fill project was formally completed on August 24, 1937.

This photograph shows the northwest view across the Yerba Buena Shoals from Yerba Buena Island on March 23, 1936, as construction of Treasure Island has just begun. U.S. dredge *Sacramento*, used to fill Yerba Buena Shoals, is shown on the far right. Angel Island is at the top center of the photograph, and Mount Tamalpais can be seen behind and to the left. (Courtesy of National Archives.)

This spectacular aerial view looking southeast shows Treasure Island beginning to blossom from Yerba Buena Shoals. Note the characteristic fill pattern formed by material flowing outward from the central flow pipe, leading from the middle, across the water, and connecting to U.S. dredge *Sacramento*. (Courtesy of National Archives.)

Looking north across the Yerba Buena Shoals from Yerba Buena Island on March 23, 1936, the camera shows construction of Treasure Island at the very beginning. U.S. hopper dredge *San Pablo* can be seen at the top left in this continuation of the panorama photograph from the opposite page. The absence of land in this view gives a fine impression of the San Francisco Bay prior to the birth of the island. (Courtesy of National Archives.)

U.S. dredge *Sacramento* makes the first fill on the southwest corner of Yerba Buena Shoals, as shown from Yerba Buena Island on March 1, 1936. U.S. hopper dredge *San Pablo* can be seen in the distant background dredging material from other areas of the San Francisco Bay to be deposited directly on the northwest section of the fill zone. (Courtesy of National Archives.)

This photograph shows the southeast view from within the fill zone on April 15, 1936. The fill being dredged is pumped with great force, as can be seen in this image. Treasure Island is literally rising from the bay. (Courtesy of National Archives.)

The business end of a dredge flow pipe pumps fill into the Yerba Buena Shoals on April 9, 1936. Over 25 million cubic yards of fill would be pumped, dredged, and dug from the bottom of San Francisco Bay in this manner to help create Treasure Island. (Courtesy of National Archives.)

This is a continuation of the panorama photograph at left taken on April 15, 1936, from the fill zone of Treasure Island. U.S. dredge *Sacramento* can be seen on the right. At the center rear of the photograph is the U.S. Navy training station located on Yerba Buena Island. (Courtesy of National Archives.)

Shown on April 23, 1936, is U.S. dredge *Multnomah* upon arrival in San Francisco for the Yerba Buena Shoals fill project. *Multnomah* was towed from Portland, Oregon, and is having its open-ocean support beams removed prior to starting work. (Courtesy of National Archives.)

On May 6, 1936, a bottom dredge at right and clamshell dredge at left continue their work, as seen from Yerba Buena Island. Treasure Island begins to take shape. (Courtesy of National Archives.)

This panoramic view from Yerba Buena Island on June 8, 1936, looks to the west. U.S. dredge *San Joaquin* is at the left building the causeway to connect Treasure Island, and U.S. dredge *Sacramento* is at right filling the southeast corner. The unfinished Golden Gate Bridge is to the rear, and high in the clouds is a blimp heading to sea. (Courtesy of National Archives.)

Dredge *Pronto* helps to fill Yerba Buena Shoals for the creation of Treasure Island. Fill was taken from the front and pumped out the rear through the flow pipe seen exiting at right. Given the power lines to the left, this image would seem to be from mid-1937, but the date is listed as July 1936. (Courtesy of National Archives.)

This photograph is a continuation of the panorama photograph at left taken on June 8, 1936, and looks north. Clamshell dredge *Monarch* is building the foundations for the island's retaining wall on the south end, while smaller constructors' derricks are building the wall itself. (Courtesy of National Archives.)

This photograph looks north along the causeway from Yerba Buena Island to the fill for Treasure Island on August 6, 1936. Various contractor derricks can be seen building the outside retaining wall for the fill, and a flow pipe for a dredge snakes toward the center. (Courtesy of National Archives.)

Treasure Island is pictured on August 27, 1936, as the fill begins to take form. Various dredges, clamshells, and contractor derricks can be seen plying around the fill zone. (Courtesy of National Archives.)

Looking southwest toward the San Francisco skyline in August 1936, California governor Frank Merriam is seen officially breaking ground on Treasure Island, while a large crowd of military, political, and social dignitaries both domestic and foreign look on. The celebration was held in the southwest corner of the island, where the main administration building would be constructed. (Courtesy of National Archives.)

This aerial view shows the advanced progress of Treasure Island on December 12, 1936. Much of the outside retaining wall has been completed, as has the ferry dock at the center of the western side. Multiple dredges continue to work to finish the fill and complete the island's formation. (Courtesy of National Archives.)

Taken in January 1937, this view to the north shows Treasure Island almost completely filled. All that remains is to fill the center region to the north. The outline of the first of two permanent aircraft hangars can be seen taking shape at the lower right. (Courtesy of National Archives.)

In this view looking north from Yerba Buena Island on February 5, 1937, the outline of the original permanent aircraft hangar can be seen to the right and the second hangar is beginning to take shape on the left. (Courtesy of National Archives.)

This view looks east from the location of the Treasure Island Administration Building toward the now-forming permanent aircraft hangars on March 4, 1937. At the center of the photograph is a rail line built to allow railcars to float across the bay in barges and move onto the fill with loads of construction material and equipment. (Courtesy of National Archives.)

The skeletal frame of the Treasure Island Administration and Air Terminal Building takes shape in this photograph looking north on March 4, 1937. A Public Works Administration building can be seen at the lower left corner. Much of the island is now filled in. (Courtesy of National Archives.)

Another aerial view shows Treasure Island under construction, this time looking south on March 20, 1937, and taken by the 88th Army Air Corps Reconnaissance Squadron. Depending on the weather and tide conditions, until the retaining wall was completed, the northern end would remain far wetter than the rest of the fill zone. (Courtesy of National Archives.)

In this impressive view looking southwest on May 1, 1937, both permanent aircraft hangars can be seen. In addition, the fill is close to being completed at the south end of the island, and rigs are preparing the soil for desalination and future building foundations. (Courtesy of National Archives.)

This photograph looks south on May 25, 1937, from Treasure Island across the causeway built to connect with Yerba Buena Island. Various grading machines can be seen working on the road surface that will connect to the Bay Bridge. (Courtesy of National Archives.)

The Treasure Island Administration and Air Terminal Building takes form in this photograph looking north taken on May 26, 1937. The frames of additional buildings not planned to be permanent can be seen to the right. (Courtesy of National Archives.)

In this aerial view taken on June 19, 1937, by the 88th Army Air Corps Reconnaissance Squadron, the now-familiar linear lines of Treasure Island can clearly be seen. At this point, the fill operations were largely complete, the retaining walls were nearly done, and several buildings were under construction. (Courtesy of National Archives.)

This view to the north from the causeway of Treasure Island is from July 8, 1937. The retaining wall and the Administration and Air Terminal Building (center) can be clearly seen. (Courtesy of National Archives.)

This photograph of the western retaining wall on Treasure Island looking north and taken on July 8, 1937, shows the precision with which the island was built and the amount of flotsam in the San Francisco Bay that day. (Courtesy of National Archives.)

This view of the western retaining wall on Treasure Island looking south was taken on July 8, 1937. This photograph was taken on the same date and in the same location as the above image but looking the opposite direction. (Courtesy of National Archives.)

No 2
Yerba Buena Projects
Shoals
...ng Suction pump
Dredge

This July 19, 1937, photograph shows a close-up view of the rear suction pump of a portable dredge used to help finish the Yerba Buena Shoals fill. The fill was dredged from the source at the front of the vessel and pumped through it and out the back, where it would exit via varying lengths of flow pipes depending on where the fill was required. The flow pipes could be rather long if needed, as witnessed by various images shown previously. (Courtesy of National Archives.)

Nº 289
Yerba Buena Projects
Shoals
Assemblying
Portable Dredge on Fill
July 19, 1937

The north end of Treasure Island is shown on July 19, 1937. The portable dredge can be seen to the left, this time from the front of the vessel. (Courtesy of National Archives.)

Looking west on July 19, 1937, this photograph shows another perspective on the portable dredge seen in the previous two images. In this view, Alcatraz can also be seen to the right. (Courtesy of National Archives.)

A final view from the north end of Treasure Island was taken on July 19, 1937. In the background, the portable dredge shown in previous images can be seen. To the right in the center is a derrick completing the rock retaining wall around the island. Over 287,000 tons of rock was used to build the retaining wall around the island in this way. (Courtesy of National Archives.)

This aerial view looks west as the fill project for Yerba Buena Shoals nears completion. The island's permanent structures can be seen at center left. Alcatraz can be seen at the upper left. The north end of the island was not deemed as stable as the south, so no permanent structures were planned, and it would become the parking lot for the Golden Gate Expo in 1939. (Courtesy of National Archives.)

Treasure Island is pictured from the causeway looking northeast on November 12, 1937. In this image, significant progress can be seen on the island, as the outlines so familiar are now all present—the Administration and Air Terminal Building and the two permanent hangars. In the foreground, workers are assembling the water supply lines to connect Treasure Island with the Bay Bridge. (Courtesy of National Archives.)

Two years after the Yerba Buena Shoals project began, construction for the Golden Gate International Expo was in full swing. This view looking north from the roof of the future Homes and Garden Building near the Court of Honor was taken in February 1938. In little more than a year, this entire view would be transformed into a magical and dynamic public attraction. Seen prominently in this view are the Douglas fir planks used to construct the temporary buildings that would be coated in colored stucco. Also seen is the rigid iron frame of the Tower of the Sun, which required pilings driven 90 feet into the soil. The tower would rise 400 feet above the San Francisco Bay when complete. (Author's collection.)

In this image taken on August 21, 1938, the Tower of the Sun is largely complete, save for interior scaffolding yet to be removed. The groundwork nearby also has yet to be completed. Trees framing the image at left and right can be seen, just two of the 4,000 that would be planted for the fair. (Author's collection.)

Two

THE GOLDEN GATE EXPO
1939–1940

World's Fairs were born from the Industrial Revolution as celebrations to highlight innovations in science and technology. World's Fairs were first seen in the mid-1800s in France and formalized in London in 1851 with the Great Exhibition, otherwise know as the Crystal Palace Exhibition. As the eras progressed, commonly held notions of what World's Fairs should represent evolved accordingly; they tended to closely follow the strands of human progress currently in vogue.

At the time of the Golden Gate International Exposition held on Treasure Island in 1939 and 1940, World's Fairs were largely viewed as places to explore issues facing humankind and to embrace cultural identity and world relations. Although science and technology played large roles in the Golden Gate Expo, also present were strong themes related to bettering society, looking to the future, cultural harmony (in this case with a special emphasis on the Pacific Basin), and utopian ideals of progress and achievement. Interwoven among these themes was also an overtly commercial element in the form of popular entertainment, souvenirs, food and drink, wares, and much more. All these things helped to create the lasting image of what the fair on Treasure Island was all about for the two years it was in operation.

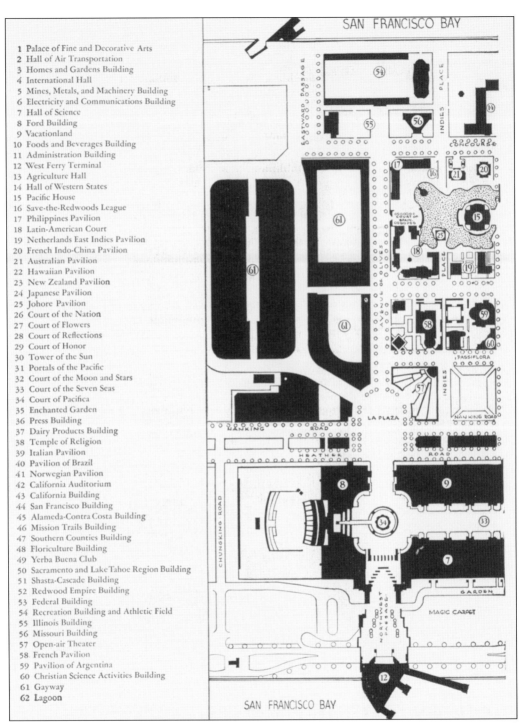

This overview map shows Treasure island as it existed during the Golden Gate International Exposition from February 1939 until September 1940. Using this map and the panoramic photograph

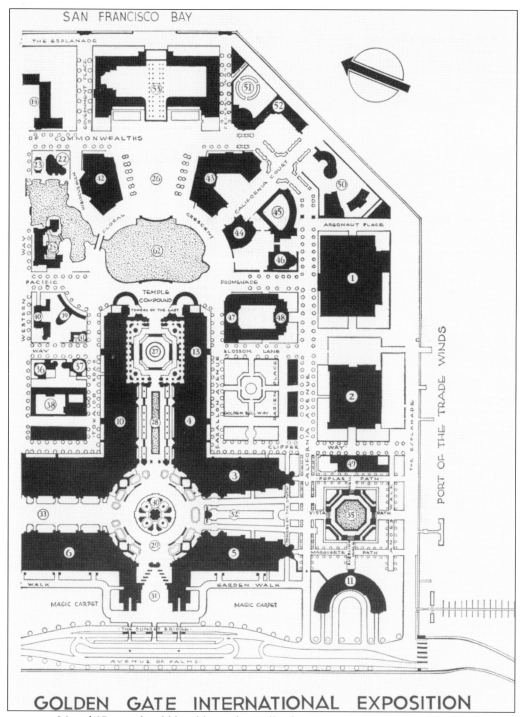

GOLDEN GATE INTERNATIONAL EXPOSITION

on pages 36 and 37, one should be able to physically place most of the images of the World's Fair shown hereafter. (Author's collection.)

An impressive aerial view of Treasure Island looks northwest and shows the layout of the Golden Gate International Exposition. The Boeing B-314 clipper (likely the *California Clipper*) is docked at the lower right with a Sikorsky S-42 clipper to the left. The parking lot, devoid of vehicles, can be seen at the north end of the island. Using this photograph and the maps on the preceding pages, one should be able to orient oneself to the location of many of the images on Treasure Island during the Golden Gate International Expo. (Courtesy of National Archives.)

This letter was sent from Treasure Island on the opening day of the fair at 9:00 a.m., February 18, 1939. This is not just a letter, it is a "first day cover" used to commemorate an event with special art and newly released stamps on the very first day they were available. The postage used is a 3¢ 1939 Golden Gate International Exposition stamp issued to commemorate the start of the fair. (Author's collection.)

This image was taken from the top of the Vacationland Building, looking south down the Court of the Seven Seas to the Court of Honor and the Tower of the Sun. On the right in the background is the Bay Bridge with Yerba Buena Island to its left. Some of the architectural details can be clearly seen on the crown of the building to the right. (Author's collection.)

This aerial view shows the Tower of the Sun rising 400 feet into the air and the Court of Honor around it. This view looks east from the Portals of the Pacific entrance at the bottom, to the Tower of the Sun, the Court of Reflections beyond, and the Arch of Triumph at the top center. The buildings immediately flanking the Court of Reflections are the Foods and Beverages Building on the left and the International Hall on the right. The Court of Honor and its immense tower were designed by architect Arthur Brown. (Author's collection.)

This photograph looks south past the base of the Tower of the Sun toward the Court of the Moon and the Treasure Garden, with its column of water rising in the distance. Yerba Buena Island is at the rear of the photograph. No less than four elaborate pools and water fountains are seen in this view. (Author's collection.)

This photograph shows the northwest view from the Homes and Gardens Building to the sculpture *Evening Star* by Ettore Cadorin in the Court of the Moon. This sculpture was one of the most beloved of the entire expo. The Tower of the Sun is on the right, and seen prominently to the fore is an example of a light post in the shape of a lyre. (Author's collection.)

Continuing the view to the left, this photograph looks southwest toward the base of the Tower of the Sun in the Court of Honor. The southernmost Elephant Tower can be seen flanking the Portals of the Pacific entrance at the far right of the photograph, with the Bay Bridge at the rear. (Author's collection.)

This photograph looks east from the roof of the Foods and Beverages Building across the Court of Reflections toward the Arch of Triumph at the entrance to the Court of Flowers. The poles seen here are lights styled as Siamese ceremonial umbrellas. The Court of Reflection and the Arch of Triumph were designed by L. P. Hobart. (Author's collection.)

Another view taken from the top of the Vacationland Building looks south down the Court of the Seven Seas to the Court of Honor and the Tower of the Sun. The Court of the Seven Seas (half of which is seen in here) was the longest in the expo at 1,000 feet end to end. It was designed by George Pelham and J. H. Clark and, according to the 1939 Expo guidebook, represented "man's conquest of the world's oceans." (Author's collection.)

The Tower of the Sun, looking west from the aptly named Court of Reflections, is captured nicely in this photograph. The Tower of the Sun contained a series of eight sculptures by William Gordon Huff, including *Industry*, *Agriculture*, *Science*, and *The Arts*. (Author's collection.)

This photograph looking east shows the approach to the south entrance via the Portals of the Pacific with the Tower of the Sun rising behind. The design of the fair took into account the prevailing weather patterns of the San Francisco Bay and resulted in both main entrances sporting an ingenious design of walls as wind baffles. (Author's collection.)

This photograph looks east toward the Portals of the Pacific entrance in 1939 while approaching Treasure Island via a Key System transit ferry. Both Elephant Towers can clearly be seen flanking the Tower of the Sun. The entrance system as described above can be seen as well, with walls rising many stories to the left and right of the wind baffle entrance. (Author's collection.)

An Elephant train sight-seeing tram passes in front of the Court of the Moon in this photograph looking north to the Tower of the Sun. These trams plied the length and width of Treasure Island, making stops along the way to pick up and drop off passengers and to describe the sights along the way. For 35¢, one could travel from the parking lot at the north end of the island to the entrances and around the interior of the fair. (Author's collection.)

The northern Elephant Tower at the Portals of the Pacific entrance is pictured. This perspective was taken outside the entrance looking southeast. Designed by Donald Macky, the towers sat atop the entrance designed by Ernest Weihe. Elephants were a widely used theme during the Golden Gate Expo, and these towers were successful examples. (Author's collection.)

A view from the outside looking north toward the Portals of the Pacific entrance is captured in this image. Fronds of one of the 4,000 trees brought to the island frame the image. A bed of one million ice plants, immune to the westerly winds, stretches along the perimeter. This was dubbed the magic carpet by visitors due to its immense size and vibrant colors. (Author's collection.)

A closer view of the Elephant Towers was taken from the Portals of the Pacific entrance. An immense bed of ice plants, stretching 25 acres around the western perimeter and dubbed the magic carpet, can also be seen in this image. (Author's collection.)

This view looks west from the Court of Flowers, past the Fountain of Life, and through the Arch of Triumph, with the Tower of the Sun obscured to the rear. The sculpture *Girl and Rainbow* by O. C. Malmquist sits atop the fountain in front of the arch. (Author's collection.)

Looking north from the Court of Flowers at the Fountain of Life, O. C. Malmquist's sculpture *Girl and Rainbow* can be seen. Malmquist also designed the prominently displayed 22-foot-tall wrought iron sculpture *Phoenix* that sat atop the Tower of the Sun. (Author's collection.)

This photograph captures the south view in the Court of Flowers of O. C. Malmquist's sculpture *Girl and Rainbow* sitting atop the Fountain of Life. This view captures the detail that went into the many fountains and sculptures that dotted the Golden Gate Expo, complete with wide arrays of flora, smaller works of art, light effects, and water displays. (Author's collection.)

This view looks west from the Court of Flowers, past the Fountain of Life, and through the Arch of Triumph, with the Tower of the Sun to the rear. The sculpture *Girl and Rainbow* by O. C. Malmquist can be seen atop the fountain in front of the arch. (Author's collection.)

This view west through the Arch of Triumph, between the Court of Flowers and the Court of Reflections, shows the Tower of the Sun in the center. The Arch of Triumph was 105 feet tall with an entrance spanning 90 feet. (Author's collection.)

SOUTH GARDENS G.G.I. EXPOSITION '39

This postcard view looks south toward Yerba Buena Island from the Tower of the Sun. The sculpture *Evening Star* by Ettore Cadorin in the Court of the Moon is directly in the center, and the Treasure Garden is just beyond. Both locations were designed by G. W. Kelham. The fountain in the Court of the Moon consisted of 24 water arcs spaced evenly throughout, whereas the fountain in the Treasure Garden was a vertical waterspout. (Author's collection.)

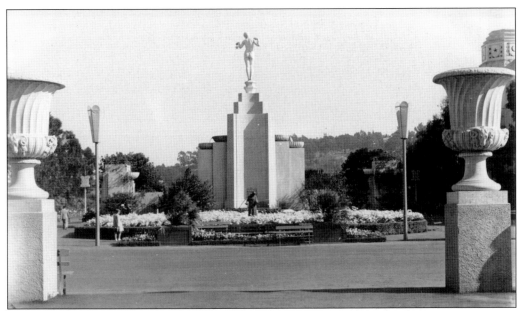

This ground-level perspective looks south toward the sculpture *Evening Star* by Ettore Cadorin in the Court of the Moon. The Tower of the Sun in the Court of Honor is directly to the photographer's rear. *Evening Star* was much beloved by visitors, although critics were lukewarm, as they were to most expo art. Today it's hard not to appreciate the works on Treasure Island, particularly in their absence 68 years later. (Author's collection.)

This photograph looks southeast from the Esplanade near the Treasure Garden across the Port of the Trade Winds toward the Oakland span of the Bay Bridge. A Sikorsky S-42 seaplane is moored at the right. The Port of the Trade Winds was a main base for famous planes like the Sikorsky S-42 and Boeing 314 clippers. (Author's collection.)

The Treasure Garden, designed by G. W. Kelham, is shown looking from south of the fountain. Yerba Buena Island can be seen to the rear. The fountain was designed to create the illusion of water both rising and falling at the same time. (Author's collection.)

Another view of the fountain in the Treasure Garden looks east. The building housing the Yerba Buena Club can be seen to the rear. The fountain was flanked by numerous sculptures, and *The Moon and the Dawn* by Ettore Cadorin is in the foreground. (Author's collection.)

This view looks north toward the fountain in the Treasure Garden from the area of the Esplanade. Beyond the fountain water spout is the Tower of the Sun. Flanking to the right and left are the elaborately detailed towers of the Court of the Moon. (Author's collection.)

This close-up view looks east over the easternmost flanking tower of the Court of the Moon. The tower was stuccoed in a vibrant color dubbed "evening star blue" and abutted directly to the building housing the Homes and Gardens display. The tower was adorned with various murals and elaborate artistic details. (Author's collection.)

The fountain in the Treasure Garden looks northeast toward the easternmost flanking tower in the Court of the Moon. The Cambodian-styled tower on the Temple of the East near Temple Compound can be seen to the far right. (Author's collection.)

This view from the Court of Honor looks northeast toward the Vacationland Building adorned with the bows of ancient ships. This is the start of the 1,000-foot Court of the Seven Seas that stretched across the length of the fair to the Court of Pacifica at the north end. (Author's collection.)

This view looks north down the Court of the Seven Seas toward the Court of Pacifica in the distance. The abundance of flora, including trees, shrubs, bushes, and a multitude of flowers, is apparent in this photograph. All vegetation had to be brought to the island and planted by hand by a workforce of 1,200. (Author's collection.)

Another view looks north down the Court of the Seven Seas toward the Court of Pacifica. This 1,000-foot-long and 200-foot-wide walkway was frequently packed with festivalgoers. (Author's collection.)

This photograph looks north along the Court of the Seven Seas toward the Court of Pacifica. Note the visitors strolling along and being carted to their next destination, while a cameraman is slightly hidden by the shadow cast from the Tower of the Sun. (Author's collection.)

This fantastic photograph was taken from the roof of the Vacationland Building looking to the north. This view captures the Court of Pacifica and shows the enormous size of Ralph Stackpole's statue *Pacifica*. The Fountain of Western Waters can be seen to the lower left. The Court of Pacifica was designed by George Pelham and J. H. Clark. (Author's collection.)

This postcard view looks north from the Court of Honor toward the Court of Pacifica. Standing 80 feet tall at the end was Ralph Stackpole's statue *Pacifica*, which was imbued as the centerpiece of the entire Golden Gate Expo. (Author's collection.)

Another postcard view looks north closer toward the Court of Pacifica. Note the continuation of the nautical theme through the use of ship riggings complete with crow's nests. This contrasts uniquely with the Eastern-themed and classically intoned architecture of the fair, much to the dismay of many critics of the era. Most visitors felt it was like a fantastic scene from an epic filmscape. (Author's collection.)

This view looks north across the Court of Pacifica and the Fountain of Western Waters to the statue *Pacifica* by Ralph Stackpole. The steps at the base of *Pacifica* led to an open-air theater where 500 human and animal actors gave three to four performances a day of *Cavalcade of the Golden West*. It was later renamed *Cavalcade of a Nation* in 1940. (Author's collection.)

Looking north toward the 80-foot-tall statue *Pacifica* by Ralph Stackpole, this view also captures the Fountain of Western Waters and a gathering of Spanish-themed dancers and musicians. Many such groups wandered the expo catering to different musical and ethnic styles. (Author's collection.)

A view from the top of the Vacationland Building gazes west across the Court of Pacifica to the northern entrance, known as the Northwest Passage. Above the entrance from the Northwest Passage is an enormous mural by the Bruton family called *The Peacemakers*. This work measured 144 feet by 58 feet and consisted of 270 different panels. (Author's collection.)

This close-up view looks north of the Fountain of Western Waters in the Court of Pacifica. Numerous sculptures were found here designed in the Pacific Unity style, which discarded classical themes and heeded a stripped-down, streamlined feel infused with "common man" elements and heroic overtones. One in particular, Cecilia Graham's *Woman Grinding Farina*, was actually considered rather controversial due to its physical position and nudity. (Author's collection.)

Looking east approaching the north entrance via the Northwest Passage, this view is directly opposite that found on page 60 and leads to the Court of Pacifica. This entrance was designed in the same manner as the southern entrance, using wind baffles to protect visitors from the harsh wind prevalent in the area. (Author's collection.)

The Fountain of Western Waters in the Court of Pacifica and the sculptures that were situated therein are pictured looking west from ground level. The mural *The Peacemakers* by the Bruton family can be seen at the rear along the western wall, which was also the entrance from the Northwest Passage. (Author's collection.)

This view north toward Ralph Stackpole's statue *Pacifica* also includes the entrance to the *Cavalcade of the Golden West* show. Running from the foot of the statue was an elaborate waterfall, and behind was a free-hanging metal prayer curtain 100 feet tall and 48 feet wide. It was designed to gently sway and tinkle in the wind. The photograph captures the imposing size of *Pacifica* contrasted against the figures standing next to it. (Author's collection.)

Another view looks north toward the statue *Pacifica* in the Court of Pacifica and the Fountain of Western Waters. (Author's collection.)

This close-up of Ralph Stackpole's *Pacifica* in the Court of Pacifica at the north end of the fair includes a 100-foot-by-48-foot free-hanging metal prayer curtain behind *Pacifica*. Efforts to stem wind within the fair resulted in a fan having to be used to generate curtain movement. (Author's collection.)

North, beyond the watchful pose of the statue of *Pacifica*, lies the wildly elaborate open-air theater where 300 actors and 200 animals took part in daily shows known as the *Cavalcade of the Golden West*. The theater is empty, presumably because this was a rehearsal. (Author's collection.)

In addition to actors and live animals, trains and wagons made an appearance on stage as well. Here the meeting of the transcontinental railway is depicted on stage, likely a first in this elaborate format. (Author's collection.)

Herds of cattle had roles in the cavalcade, as did riders on horseback, pictured overlooking the stage in the simulated Sierra Nevada Mountains at rear. (Author's collection.)

Shown are the flags of the many nations that made America great, as included in the cavalcade performance. The actors' speaking parts were one aspect that was not overly strong; of the 300 actors, only 9 were responsible for the dialogue, which was broadcast over loudspeakers representing hundreds of separate parts. Close up, the effect must have been somewhat less than convincing. (Author's collection.)

This photograph looks east from the Vacationland Building along the Court of the Seven Seas to the exhibit and concessions area of Central Square and La Plaza. Just beyond is the Gayway, which was the carnival and amusement-park area of the expo. (Author's collection.)

This view shows the eastern view across La Plaza towards the Gayway. Numerous vendors and booths in this area sold every kind of food, trinket, and oddity one could imagine. The exhibits here tended toward the carnivalesque, and many were rather risqué given the era, live nudity included. The Ghirardelli Chocolate Building is at the top left, and the full-service and well-stocked Owl Drugs was to its right. (Author's collection.)

This photograph looks southeast from the roof of the Vacationland Building across Central Square toward the numerous festival groupings in the distance. (Author's collection.)

A closer view of La Plaza looks east toward the entrance to the Gayway. Numerous Elephant trains can be seen plying along beside various vendors. The Ghirardelli Chocolate Building is in the top center of the image. Take note of the roller coaster in the Gayway at the top left. (Author's collection.)

A ground-level view of the La Plaza area looks east toward the Ghirardelli Chocolate Building and Owl Drugs. The Gayway was located to the left. Note the disheveled and well-visited feel the grounds have, which give the impression of a late summer afternoon after a ball game in San Francisco. (Author's collection.)

Numerous visitors busily pass through the La Plaza area, and Elephant trains take passengers to and fro in this southeast view. A constant theme of many images from this era can be clearly witnessed here: dressing up wasn't a just a thing done on Sunday—men and boys were in suits and ladies and girls in dresses. (Author's collection.)

The J. Varsi Company booth can be seen to the left, and at the center rear is the National Cash Register Building in this view looking east in the La Plaza area. As the name states, this building housed a giant cash register that displayed a running total of the day's visitors. One has to wonder how much cash they kept in a till that size. (Author's collection.)

The National Cash Register Building displayed the number of visitors each day, as recorded every 30 minutes. At the date and time this image was taken, 124,043 people had come to the expo. This cash register was over two stories tall and not, as this perspective might indicate, table-top size; each number was over two feet tall. (Author's collection.)

A crowd of festival attendees relaxes at the base of the National Cash Register Building. In this image, take note of the number of men wearing fedoras. One never tires of contrasting the differences between 1939 and the current era. (Author's collection.)

This view looks south from the Gayway toward the Bay Bridge in the distance, taken from one of the Gayway amusement rides. Directly in the foreground is the Happy Valley Ranch, a place of ill repute but very well visited. In the distance, the Pacific Basin area can be seen in addition to the Federal Building and Hall of Western States. (Author's collection.)

This view from the same Gayway amusement ride looks southwest with the San Francisco skyline in the distance. The Tower of the Sun is at left, the Gayway can be seen arrayed below, and the National Cash Register Building is to the right. This image gives a perspective of the many photographs seen previously but from the far northeast corner of the island looking back. (Author's collection.)

The Gayway itself is shown looking directly east down the main avenue through the amusement area. Many carnival locations can be seen, including the famous Sally Rand's Nude Ranch. Also seen are the Hams and Bacon shop and a penny arcade. (Author's collection.)

The Gayway amusement area included dual Ferris wheels and the exciting motorcycle-rider-in-cage spectacle. The amusement area also housed a roller coaster, a giant multistory cage ride, bumper cars, and numerous other thrilling ventures in addition to food, trinkets, and oddities. (Author's collection.)

The venerable Goodyear blimp floats over Treasure Island during the Golden Gate Expo, providing an amazing birds-eye view of the fair. (Author's collection.)

This photograph from March 19, 1939, shows the multistory pagoda from within the Chinese Village, located near the Gayway. The Chinese Village housed numerous exhibits and displays relating to China and served Chinese food and sold Chinese-related wares and trinkets. The pagoda was impressively detailed, given its relatively temporary nature. (Author's collection.)

The Netherlands East Indies Pavilion within the Pacific Basin area near the center of Treasure Island is pictured from the east. This building housed displays on all the islands in the region including Bali, Java, Celebes, and Borneo. An aquarium of regional tropical fish was present as well. (Author's collection.)

The Pacific Basin area is shown in this view to the northeast. The Japanese Pavilion is in the center and the Netherlands East Indies Building is to its left. An Elephant train moves through the crowd. (Author's collection.)

A parade of Japanese children stands in ceremonial garb near the Pacific Basin area. The Japanese Pavilion seen to the rear combined feudal Japanese architecture, a Samurai house, and a Buddhist temple. Its elaborate layout included a Japanese garden, bridge, and 4,000 traditional lanterns. (Author's collection.)

Another view of the same parade in the Pacific Basin area includes Japanese women in traditional kimonos passing by the camera. Displays in the Japanese Pavilion included the history and manufacture of silk, the history of ancient and modern Japan, and Japanese religions. (Author's collection.)

The Johore Pavilion in the Pacific Basin is shown in this east view. Johore is on the Malaysian peninsula. In a move directly in conflict with the theme of Pacific Unity that was the foundation for the entire expo, the Japanese occupied Johore in 1942 during the war in the Pacific. Note Treasure Island expo workers patching the walkway to the left while visitors enter the exhibit in the center. (Author's collection.)

A view of the largest tree in the world, nicknamed "General Sherman," is seen on display in the Pacific Basin area at the Life History of the Redwoods Building. (Author's collection.)

Another view of the Johore Pavilion shows the Pacific Basin area of the expo. Inside were displays on daily life, animals native to the region, handiwork, traditional clothing, and natural resources. (Author's collection.)

This north view from near the Temple Compound looks out across the lagoon known as the Lake of the Nations toward the Pacific Basin area. The Japanese Pavilion is on the right, the Italian Pavilion can be seen to the left behind the structure with the clock, and the northernmost tower of the Temple of the East is on the far left. (Author's collection.)

This postcard view looks southwest from the Lake of the Nations to the Temple Compound and the southern tower of the Temple of the East. Temple Compound was designed by William Merchant. The two bas-relief works to the left and right are *Path of Darkness* (left) by Lulu Braghetta and *Dance of Life* (right) by Jacques Schnier. The sign at center proclaims "Folies Bergere, 50 French Beauties at the California Auditorium." (Author's collection.)

The Temple of the East in the Temple Compound is pictured. The bas-relief *Dance of Life* by Jacques Schnier can be seen on the wall to the left. The Lake of the Nations is directly behind the camera in this image. (Author's collection.)

The Lake of the Nations looks east toward the Federal Building in this photograph. The Lake of the Nations was an interior lagoon connecting the area of the California Group of Buildings, Temple Compound, and the Pacific Basin via a shallow waterway. Seen on the Federal Building at the rear are two large murals, *The Conquering of the West by Water* and *The Conquering of the West by Land*, by Herman Volz and completed by WPA artists. (Author's collection.)

Another view of the Federal Building looks northeast near the Lake of the Nations, the Court of Nations, and the California Group of Buildings. (Author's collection.)

This photograph looks northeast across the Lake of the Nations toward the State of California Auditorium. Numerous radio broadcasts were conducted here, with thousands presented during the fair. Radio broadcasts could be heard throughout the island transmitted from this location. The building included four studios with public seating, including one with over 3,500 seats. (Author's collection.)

This close-up view looks east on one of the Federal Building murals. The Federal Building housed numerous exhibits, including sections on Native Americans, conservation, social affairs, science, the WPA, the Coast Guard, and many others. This building burned to the ground on August 24, 1940, just days before the fair ended, killing a firefighter in the process. (Author's collection.)

80

This photograph of the Lake of the Nations faces southeast toward the building that housed the State of California and San Francisco exhibits. The crowds at the foreground are assembled on the steps of the Temple Compound area, where an outdoor band shell was located, providing big-name performances on a regular basis. (Author's collection.)

Another perspective looks southeast of the Temple Compound area toward the California and San Francisco exhibits and the Bay Bridge in the distance. (Author's collection.)

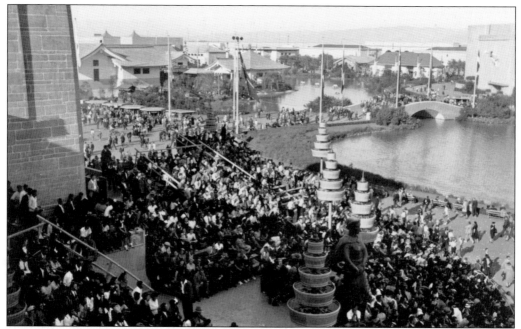

High atop the steps of the Temple of the East, this photographer captured the view eastward toward the Pacific Basin. The bridge across the lagoon connecting the Lake of the Nations to the Pacific Basin area can be seen at right. The crowds are awaiting a performance at the band shell out of view to the right of this photograph. (Author's collection.)

Pictured is the outdoor seating area near the Temple Compound on the western side of the Lake of the Nations. Playing the band shell with his jazz band is Freddy Martin, nicknamed "Mr. Silvertone" and a very popular performer with expo crowds. (Author's collection.)

This view looks south from the top of the seating area in the Temple Compound, overlooking the southern end of the Lake of the Nations and the San Francisco Building on the right. To the left is the Mission Trails Building, which housed displays highlighting the history and design of missions in California. (Author's collection.)

Another southeast view from the Temple Compound includes the band shell and the Lake of the Nations. Playing for the crowd is none other than William Bassie, better known to many as Count Bassie. He is seen performing with the Count Bassie Orchestra. (Author's collection.)

The Hall of Flowers is seen from the rear in the area of the California Group of Buildings on the southeastern corner of Treasure Island. The exterior covering of the building was made of non-transparent cellophane to act as a giant greenhouse, and the interior housed hundreds of rare and exotic flowers on display from around the world. (Author's collection.)

The Redwood Empire Building was located at the extreme southeast corner of Treasure Island near the California Group of Buildings. This pavilion housed displays highlighting the California Redwood and included many live native redwoods. (Author's collection.)

This unique photograph shows the view southwest toward the Mission Trails Building. The exterior of the building housing the San Francisco Pavilion can be seen to the right. All across the expo, one could find alcoves and places to explore and view the architecture of the island. (Author's collection.)

This is a view south toward the Mission Trails Building. The Southern Counties Building is on the right, and behind it to the rear is the Palace of Fine and Decorative Arts, housed in the easternmost of the permanent island hangar buildings. (Author's collection.)

A look south reveals the Tower of the Sun and the Court of the Seven Seas from the steps of the Court of Pacifica. The fair ended September 29, 1940, and much of that pictured gave way for the needs of a nation gearing for a conflict in the Pacific, ironically the very same region the expo was meant to show was at peace and unity. (Author's collection.)

This ground-level view from the Fountain of Western Waters in the Court of Pacifica includes the Court of the Seven Seas toward the Tower of the Sun. The view today is very different from this same location. It will likely never again strike such a dramatic composition as that afforded by the contrasting and enduring art and architecture of the Golden Gate International Exposition. (Author's collection.)

Three

THE GOLDEN GATE EXPO
NIGHT VIEWS

One of the most stunning details of the Golden Gate International Exposition on Treasure Island was the lighting effects. Nearly $2 million was spent to layer the expo grounds with thousands of spotlights, tube lights, ultraviolet lights, fluorescent lights, and sodium vapor lights. The Panama-Pacific Exposition of 1915 in San Francisco had helped pioneer the use of night-lighting effects, but it was the Golden Gate Expo that truly took the art to a new level. Whereas the Panama-Pacific Expo had utilized mainly white lighting effects, the Golden Gate Expo introduced modern lighting in numerous colors. Lighting was used extensively to highlight the art and architecture of the island and to provide ambiance, natural lighting, mood lighting, and spotlighting to attract attention. Lights were placed in fountains, behind trees and shrubs, in beds of flowers, on top of buildings, and behind walls. They provided the visual impact of fireworks with the semi-permanence of a work of art. Many visitors to the expo marveled at the light displays, from the smallest hidden highlights to the grandest spotlights on the Tower of the Sun.

Seen at night is a tower in the Court of the Moon looking north toward the Tower of the Sun. At night, the expo exploded in an array of illuminated color harmonies and contrasts. A total of $2 million was spent on lighting effects that used a palette of seven colors to bathe every prominent feature in some form of colorful light. The tower here would have been lit with amber, rose pink, and rose red. (Author's collection.)

The Tower of the Sun was extensively lit with amber, white, green, and red. The colors changed and shifted in places, and highlighting was used extensively. Mica in the stuccoed walls added to the reflective quality of the buildings. (Author's collection.)

This view looks west from the Court of Flowers and through the Arch of Triumph to the Tower of the Sun and highlights the Fountain of Life and *Girl and Rainbow* at night. The colors here would have been cast from spotlights, tube lights, mercury lights, and other light sources in mauve, pink, white, and green. The effect was nothing short of spectacular. (Author's collection.)

This night view looks south from the steps of the Court of Pacifica down the Court of the Seven Seas to the Tower of the Sun in the distance. Spotlights cast powerful light beams around the tower that were seen all across the Bay Area. The Fountain of Western Waters was lit with lighting that changed colors and cast a luminescent glow. (Author's collection.)

This view looks north past the fountain in the Treasure Garden toward the Court of the Moon and the Tower of the Sun. The twin towers of the Court of the Moon are seen to the left and right. The Treasure Garden area had more open space, and therefore the lighting was subdued so as not to interfere with the dramatic lighting on the larger buildings. (Author's collection.)

The Tower of the Sun is pictured at the Portals of the Pacific entrance to the fair. The twin Elephant Towers flanking the Tower of the Sun were some of the most elaborately lit of the entire event. The length of the western exterior wall of the expo was bathed in white light so as to be highly visible from San Francisco, while the interior spaces closer to fair visitors used more subdued and chromatic colors for effect. (Author's collection.)

The Court of Pacifica is pictured looking north from the Fountain of Western Waters. The fountain was elaborately colored, and *Pacifica* was impressively lit by powerful spotlights. The prayer curtain hanging behind the statue was infused with layers of changing colors. (Author's collection.)

Enormous spotlights were arrayed fan-like from the Recreation Building and stadium complex in the Pacific Basin. This complex could sit 11,000 visitors and was frequently the site of light shows. (Author's collection.)

The Tower of the Sun is pictured from the fountain in the Court of the Moon. The fountain here, with 24 equally spaced water spouts, was lit with numerous spotlights and accent lighting, and the overall color palette was blue and mauve, giving the area a soft, cool effect. (Author's collection.)

Four

THE GOLDEN GATE EXPO
TRANSPORTATION

The 1939 and 1940 Golden Gate International Exposition on Treasure Island was very popular among tourists and local folk alike. Millions visited the expo during the nearly two years it was open on Treasure Island, and all had to get there by car, train, boat, or plane. The new Bay Bridge connected the fair via a causeway along Yerba Buena Island for those who were inclined to drive. They paid a toll to exit the bridge and to park on the island. For those not interested in driving, buses and trains took visitors from all parts of the Bay Area to the Oakland ferry docks or San Francisco ferry terminal. From both locations, riders could board a ferry for a few cents each and enjoy a cruise to the ferry docks on the eastern or western edge of the island. Ferry schedules during the time of the expo were frequent, making travel to Treasure Island affordable and easy going. For the more adventurous, visitors could arrive at Treasure Island via the seaplane located in the Port of the Trade Winds on the southern end of the island. This port, now known as Clipper Cove, was home to the Panama Pacific airlines clipper service. Private boats could also dock in this area for a small fee. Once on the island, travel was by foot, cart, rickshaw, or Elephant train.

This view from San Francisco proper looks east toward the ferry building. It was from here that San Francisco passengers could use the Key System ferry service to reach Treasure Island. The Key System operated inter–Bay Area transit routes including rail, bus, and ferry until the 1950s, when it was dismantled and largely taken over by AC Transit. (Author's collection.)

This view from Coit Tower in San Francisco looks east across the Embarcadero toward Treasure Island on the left and Yerba Buena Island on the right. Key System ferries would travel from the San Francisco Ferry Building across the bay to Treasure Island, bringing thousands of visitors to the island each day. Visitors could also cross the newly constructed Bay Bridge at right and park on the island. (Courtesy of John Harder collection.)

A Key System ferry heading to Treasure Island was often packed with passengers. Key System ferries made runs to Treasure Island every 10 to 20 minutes, sometimes quicker, from both the Oakland mole and the San Francisco Embarcadero. The cost was between 5¢ and 10¢ per ride, and passengers debarked on the western or eastern side of the island depending on whence they came. The last ferry from Treasure Island left around 2:30 a.m., depending on the day. (Courtesy of John Harder collection.)

This view from the west includes passengers arriving on Treasure Island from a Key System ferry docked at the western ferry landing. Once docked, passengers could purchase tickets if they didn't already have access, proceed east through the Northwest Passage, and enter the fair in the area of the Court of Pacifica. (Author's collection.)

For those not interested or able to take a Key System ferry to Treasure Island, travel by car was allowed. Tolls of 50¢ were instituted for all vehicles, and parking was available at the north end of the island for an additional 25¢ to 50¢. This view looking southwest shows the causeway leading down from the Bay Bridge to the island toll plaza. (Author's collection.)

This north-facing view shows the 12,000-car parking lot located at the north of Treasure Island. Parking fees were 25¢ to 50¢ per vehicle. A service station was available on the island in the parking area for motorists that required mechanical assistance. (Author's collection.)

Here is an example of a parking check given to motorists when the arrived on the island to park their vehicle. The cost ran between 25¢ and 50¢. (Author's collection.)

	NO 00936				
A-1	N-2	O-1	O-2	O-3	H-2
A-2	**IMPORTANT**				H-3
A-3					I-1
B-1	**MARK YOUR CHECK** with the section in which you have parked, for your convenience				I-2
B-2					I-3
B-3	**PARKING FEE 25c**				J-1
C-1	**AUTO PARK**				J-2
C-2	THIS TICKET LICENSES THE HOLDER TO PARK ONE AUTOMOBILE IN THIS AREA				J-3
C-3					K-1
D-1	**LOCK YOUR CAR**				K-2
D-2	The acceptance of this ticket constitutes an agreement between Bay Auto Parks, Inc., and the acceptor hereof, that Bay Auto Parks, Inc., shall not be responsible for loss or damage to vehicles, accessories or the contents thereof caused by fire, theft, collision, water or other causes beyond its control				K-3
D-3					L-1
E-1					L-2
E-2					L-3
E-3	**BAY AUTO PARKS** TREASURE ISLAND				M-1
F-1					M-2
F-2	GOLDEN GATE INTERNATIONAL EXPOSITION				M-3
F-3	AC 652			8	N-1
G-1	G-2	G-3	H-1		

When traveling from the East Bay to Treasure Island, visitors could take a Key System bus to the Oakland mole, where they would board a ferry bound for the eastern side of the island. This Key System bus No. 802 is marked with an X to indicate it will take riders to the expo ferry service. This particular bus is on the Hopkins line in 1940, now renamed MacArthur Boulevard. (Courtesy of John Harder collection.)

In addition to Key System bus routes, riders could also take a train to the Oakland mole. This is Key System train No. 156 marked "X Line" at the Southern Pacific underpass in Oakland in 1939. (Courtesy of John Harder collection.)

This view captures a Key System train heading down the Oakland mole directly under the newly constructed Bay Bridge. Trains would arrive at the Key System ferry terminal at the end of the

This photograph shows the Key System train terminal at the ferry docks at the end of the Oakland mole. Passengers would disembark from this location and board a ferry bound for Treasure Island or San Francisco every 10 minutes. (Courtesy of John Harder collection.)

mole, where they could board ferries bound for Treasure Island or points beyond. (Courtesy of John Harder collection.)

This view of the Bay Area highlights the technical and engineering projects that took San Francisco into the modern age. Treasure Island and the Golden Gate and Bay Bridges are all in view. This perspective looks west from the Oakland mole at the bottom, toward Treasure Island and Yerba Buena Island in the center, and San Francisco in the distance. This remarkably modern view was taken more than 60 years ago, yet the now-familiar bridges connect all points of the San Francisco Bay, which at the time was a remarkable human achievement. (Author's collection.)

The Key System ferry and train terminal at the end of the Oakland mole is shown as it appeared under the newly constructed span of the Bay Bridge. Riders could take a train from all points in the East Bay to this terminal and board a ferry bound for Treasure Island. Ferry travel was widely used during this era, particularly since before the construction of the Bay Bridge it was the only way to get from one side of the San Francisco Bay to the other. (Courtesy of John Harder collection.)

This photograph looks toward the parking area at the north end of Treasure Island as an Elephant train approaches with a load of riders. Riders could board an Elephant train for 35¢ and travel to various points all across the island. Of particular note in this image is that most everyone appears to be in relatively good spirits, though maybe not unusual for those about to enter a festival full of exciting and interesting things to do and see. (Courtesy of John Harder collection.)

This close up view shows an Elephant train on Treasure Island at night. These trains were in actuality period motorcars festooned with design elements making them appear elephant-like. Each Elephant train pulled a series of passenger carts behind them likewise festooned to appear oriental in theme. (Courtesy of John Harder collection.)

GOLDEN GATE INTERNATIONAL EXPOSITION
1940 - TREASURE ISLAND - 1940

SOUVENIR OF

ELEPHANT TRAIN

SIGHT-SEEING TOUR

FORM X-40   INTRA MURAL SERVICE

T 179448   35c

This souvenir ticket stub is from a ride on the Elephant train that shuttled passengers around Treasure Island during the 1939–1940 Golden Gate International Exposition. (Author's collection.)

A Pan American Airways Boeing B-314A clipper, named the *California Clipper*, is docked at the Pan American seaplane base in the Port of the Trade Winds to the south of Treasure Island. (Courtesy of Bill Larkins collection.)

A Pan American Airways Martin M-130 clipper named the *Philippine Clipper* is docked in Hawaii. Although not photographed at Treasure Island in this image, *Philippine Clipper* is one of only three M-130s flown by Pan American and was frequently seen there. Sadly this craft crashed into a mountain in Boonville, California, on January 21, 1943, killing all 19 on board. (Author's collection.)

A Pan American Airways Martin M-130 clipper, named the *China Clipper*, is shown as it is hoisted ashore at the Port of the Trade Winds to the south of Treasure Island. Only three of these planes were ever made. To the public, "China Clipper" became a generic name and was applied to all three Martin M-130s in Pan Am's fleet. Later the name was even extended to the Boeing B-314s. (Courtesy of Bill Larkins collection.)

A Pan American Airways Boeing B-314A clipper named the *Honolulu Clipper* takes off from the Pan American seaplane base in the Port of the Trade Winds to the south of Treasure Island. (Courtesy of Bill Larkins collection.)

The Sikorsky S-39 seaplane was based on the eastern side of Treasure Island during the expo and was operated by Paul Mantz for tours. Prior to the expo, Mantz had served as a technical advisor to Amelia Earhart on her record-breaking flight attempts. They had a parting of ways over professional differences in the spring of 1937, four months before Earhart disappeared. (Courtesy of Bill Larkins collection.)

PAUL MANTZ SEAPLANE BASE
TREASURE ISLAND
THIS SOUVENIR TICKET CERTIFIES THAT

ON THIS DATE

M

HAS FLOWN OVER THE GOLDEN GATE—ALCATRAZ—WORLD'S GREATEST BRIDGES—SAN FRANCISCO AND HAS SEEN TREASURE ISLAND IN ALL ITS BEAUTY FROM THE AIR IN ONE OF OUR GIANT TWIN-MOTOR AMPHIBIANS.

PAUL MANTZ SEAPLANE BASE
Paul Mantz, President.

This ticket stub was from a sight-seeing tour over the San Francisco Bay operated by Paul Mantz. He flew Sikorsky S-39 and S-38 seaplanes based on the eastern side of Treasure Island during the expo from 1939 to 1940. (Courtesy of Bill Larkins collection.)

This view looks east toward the Berkeley Hills from the eastern shore of Treasure Island, where Paul Mantz operated a seaplane base. The plane shown here is a Sikorsky S-38 approaching the seaplane ramp after a flight around the San Francisco Bay. (Courtesy of Bill Larkins collection.)

A night exposure looks east of a Sikorsky S-38 operated by Paul Mantz while on the seaplane ramp. The Sikorsky S-38 was a twin-engine seaplane slightly larger than the S-39. (Courtesy of Bill Larkins collection.)

A U.S. Army Air Corp Boeing YB-17 bomber is parked on display in front of the Federal Building on Treasure Island in 1940. The YB-17 was the precursor to the wildly successful B-17 *Flying Fortress*, which saw service in every theater during World War II and was a mainstay of the American bomber fleet. (Courtesy of Bill Larkins collection.)

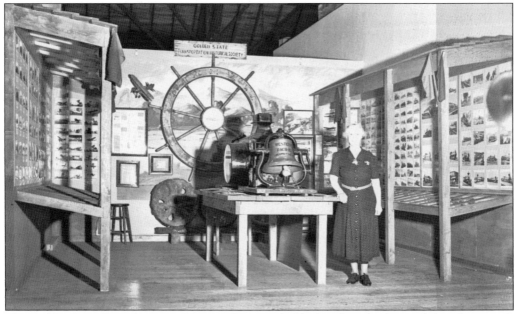

The Golden State Transportation Historical Society held a booth at the fair, and this photograph shows their display in 1940. Historian and aviation enthusiast Bill Larkins helped out at the fair with this display and took this photograph at the time. Larkins kindly provided this photograph for use in a wonderful gesture to help preserve local Bay Area history. (Courtesy of Bill Larkins collection.)

On display in the Ford Building on Treasure Island during the fair was this historic automobile, a Ford racecar named 999 after a locomotive of the period. This racecar was credited with helping to launch the career of Henry Ford and the Ford Motor Company. (Author's collection.)

This postcard highlights the traffic layout for vehicles traveling to Treasure Island from the Bay Bridge. At the time of the expo in 1939, the upper deck of the Bay Bridge was used for traffic in both directions; thus vehicles coming from San Francisco would exit east of the Yerba Buena tunnel, and those coming from the East Bay would exit west of the tunnel. (Author's collection.)

Looking north across the Trade Winds Lagoon on August 9, 1939, this view shows the Matson luxury liner docked at the south end of Treasure Island. The ship was visiting the fair to help promote Matson Day at the fair, one of dozens of such special event days held during the Golden Gate Expo. (Author's collection.)

Another view looks across the Trade Winds Lagoon, this time stepping back to before the fair opened, when the main buildings where still under construction, as can be seen in the background of the photograph. In the foreground, a Pan American clipper is towed in by a harbor craft. (Author's collection.)

Five

NAVAL STATION
TREASURE ISLAND
1941–1997

The United States Navy took over Treasure Island after the Golden Gate Expo ended in September 1940. What was planned to be the location of the new San Francisco airport instead became a major Pacific Coast naval base. At first, the navy leased the island, but on April 17, 1942, formal control was assumed entirely by the federal government. During World War II, Naval Station Treasure Island was home to numerous functions, including a massive receiving station for incoming and (mainly) outgoing troops, naval training schools, harbor patrol units, a section base, coast watchers, mine patrol forces, net tenders, and much more. When the Japanese attacked the United States on December 7, 1941, Treasure Island was thrust into the fore of the war in Pacific. Most who served in the Pacific theater passed through Treasure Island.

After World War II ended in August 1945, Naval Station Treasure Island (NSTI) continued to serve as a vital U.S. Navy base. In February 1954, the island was opened to the public for the first time since the expo ended for a much-celebrated open house that featured ship and base tours as well as a Golden Gate International Expo reunion. All through the 1950s and 1960s, NSTI continued to serve as a receiving station, training base, and homeport for various warships. During these busy times, base buildings were added and torn down, commands came and went, units were established, ships docked and left port, and thousands of men and women came to the island and served.

On May 8, 1997, Naval Station Treasure Island lowered its flag for the last time. The island was given back to the control of San Francisco in September 1997. Treasure Island now awaits the next chapter in its exciting and notable history.

A United Stated Navy Douglas SBD Dauntless dive-bomber flies over Treasure Island during World War II. This plane was the main dive-bomber of the navy between 1940 and 1943. On Treasure Island, the changes since the expo can clearly be seen, including the Naval Auxiliary Air Facility landing strip at the north end used as a forward base for antisubmarine patrols on the approaches to San Francisco Bay. (Author's collection.)

With World War II underway, tens of thousands of sailors passed through Treasure Island on their way to all points in the Pacific Theater. To help with the huge influx of servicemen, every available space on the island was put to use, including the permanent aircraft hangars, where hundreds could be housed, as seen in this photograph. (Author's collection.)

This photograph shows servicemen leaving the Treasure Island non-denominational church, constructed in July 1943. The building is still present on the island and will likely be preserved during any future island development projects. Over 2,200 weddings were conducted in this church between 1943 and 1946. (Author's collection.)

Pictured is the interior of the navy church on Treasure Island during World War II. The navy chaplain staff of this church conducted services for all faiths, helped with baptisms, loaned out their choir, presided over ship launchings, helped console tens of thousands of servicemen, and tended to the needs of prisoners of war held on the island. (Author's collection.)

A naval turret was erected for training purposes during World War II behind the first hangar at Treasure Island. This training turret still stands in the same location today and can be seen by curious visitors who look closely as they drive by. (Author's collection.)

Crews trained on Treasure Island for service aboard merchant vessels that required naval service crews for protection. (Author's collection.)

During World War II, a naval formation stands at attention in the main parade ground where the Tower of the Sun once stood. In 1947, the building at the top of the photograph (the Foods and Beverages Building during the fair) would completely burn to the ground. (Author's collection.)

Taking a step back, this photograph was taken in the area of the Federal Building at the southeast corner of Treasure Island and shows the U.S. Army "Treasure Island Company" of the 30th Infantry Regiment in parade formation. Although not taken during the naval base era, this is an excellent view of the military presence on Treasure Island during the time of the Golden Gate Expo. This unit would later help fight a massive fire on the island that consumed the California Building on August 24, 1940. (Author's collection.)

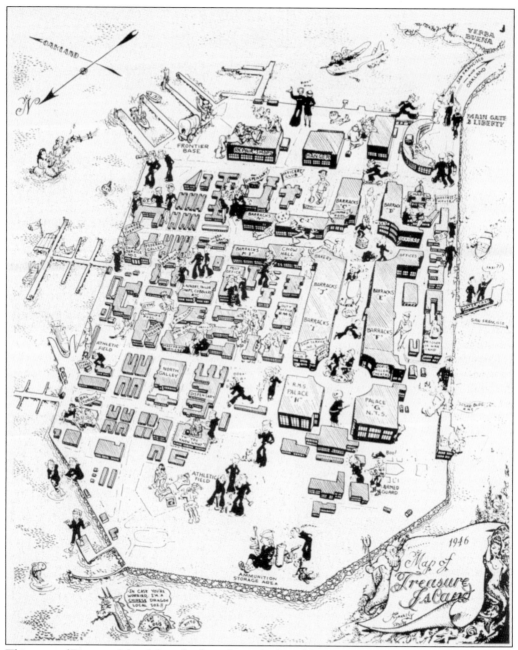

This map of Treasure Island dates back to the end of World War II in 1946. Things have changed dramatically from the time of the fair in 1939–1940. Some of the main buildings along the old Court of the Seven Seas are still present, as are the permanent administration building and hangars, but most everything else was long since removed by the time this map was drawn to make way for the navy. (Author's collection.)

This stunning image taken from downtown San Francisco captures a massive fire that broke out on Treasure Island on April 10, 1947. The fire was centered in the building formerly housing the Vacationland, Foods and Beverages, and Festival Pavilions during the time of the World's Fair. The building remained after the fair ended and was being used by the navy for many purposes, including the largest mess hall in the country. (Author's collection.)

Shown is another view of the devastating fire on Treasure Island on April 10, 1947. The fire started in an area housing a bakery and burned for days, destroying a six-block area of the island in the process. (Author's collection.)

This photograph looks north from Yerba Buena Island toward Naval Station Treasure Island in 1955. Only the three main buildings built before the expo still remain: the administration building at left and the two hangars at right. By this time, nearly every other space on the island had been transformed multiple times. To the extreme right, off the side of the image, were multiple docks for naval warships. (Courtesy of National Archives.)

Members of the U.S. Navy Treasure Island baseball team pose with a female sailor in front of the main administration building in 1955. (Courtesy of National Archives.)

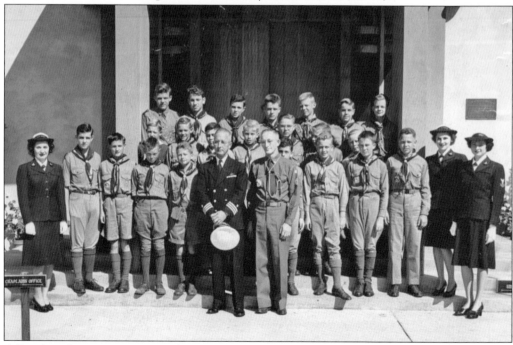

A Bay Area Scout troop poses with a naval officer in the 1950s in front of the non-denominational church erected in 1943. Hundreds of requests were made to visit the navy base by many different groups, including many Scouts who were allowed to use the world-class pool at Treasure Island during their visits. (Author's collection.)

Looking southeast towards Treasure Island in 1939, the aircraft carrier USS *Lexington* can be seen moored in the San Francisco Bay. At the time of the World's Fair, Treasure Island wasn't directly related to the navy, but San Francisco Bay had been a prominent location for navy ships for many years. During World War II, on May 8, 1942, USS *Lexington* was sunk in the Battle of the Coral Sea by Japanese Forces. (Author's collection.)

Fleet returns to San Francisco

The U.S. First Fleet arrives in San Francisco on September 9, 1960. USS *Midway* is in the lead of this long line of naval ships. At the time, three aircraft carriers called San Francisco Bay home. Many other ships were based here as well, including various destroyers and smaller vessels at Treasure Island specifically. (Author's collection.)

This image captures the stunning sight of a mushroom cloud on Treasure Island on September 27, 1957. The mushroom cloud was caused by a mock nuclear explosion that was detonated by the navy for demonstration and training purposes. A series of mock nuclear explosions took place on Treasure Island in the fall of 1957, much to the amazement and interest of Bay Area residents, in particular those on the Bay Bridge at the time of the explosions. No harm was done during these tests, as they weren't radioactive and used common explosive materials to create similar conditions in miniature scale for the navy to observe, document, and study. (Courtesy of San Francisco History Center, San Francisco Public Library.)

This is USS *Marysville* PCE-857 as seen docked at Naval Station Treasure Island in 1965. *Marysville* was laid down in 1943, launched in 1944, and commissioned into the navy as a patrol craft on April 26, 1945. In 1949, the ship had its weapons removed and was converted into an underwater electronic research vessel to be used for conducting oceanographic research and underwater sound experiments in the Pacific Ocean. (Courtesy of John Harder collection.)

USS *Koiner* DER-331 and USS *Thrasher* MSC-203 are docked at Naval Station Treasure Island on February 27, 1964. *Koiner* was laid down in July 1943, launched in October 1943, and commissioned in December 1943. *Koiner* served during World War II in the Atlantic as a destroyer escort. After the war ended, *Koiner* was decommissioned and served as a Coast Guard vessel, only to be recommissioned during the cold war to serve as a naval picket ship and early-warning craft off the coast of California. *Koiner* was stricken from the navy in 1968. *Thrasher* was a minesweeper commissioned in February 1955. *Thrasher* was stricken from the navy in 1975. (Courtesy of John Harder collection.)

USS *Walton* DE-361 and USS *Laws* DD-558 are docked at Naval Station Treasure Island on February 27, 1964. *Walton* was laid down in March 1944, launched in May 1944, and commissioned in September 1944. *Walton* served in the Pacific during World War II. In this photograph, the vessel was being used as a reserve training ship for naval personnel on Treasure Island. *Walton* was stricken from the navy in 1968. *Laws* was commissioned in November 1943 and served in the Pacific during World War II. In this photograph, the ship was also serving as a reserve training ship. *Laws* was stricken from the navy in 1973. (Courtesy of John Harder collection.)

USS *Tracer* AGR-15 is pictured docked at Naval Station Treasure Island in 1964. *Tracer* was laid down as Liberty ship *William J. Riddle* in December 1944, launched in January 1945, and commissioned shortly after. In May 1957, the ship was converted to a radar picket ship, modified for radar picket duty to detect Soviet aircraft and vessels well in advance of reaching U.S. shores, and renamed *Interrupter*. In 1959, the ship was renamed *Tracer*. *Tracer* was stricken from the navy in 1965. (Courtesy of John Harder collection.)

USS *Finch* DER-328 is docked at Naval Station Treasure Island in 1964. *Finch* was laid down in June 1943, launched in August 1943, and commissioned in December 1943. *Finch* was commissioned three separate times, lastly in August 1956 as a radar picket destroyer escort. *Finch* was stricken from the navy in 1974. (Courtesy of John Harder collection.)

A U.S. Navy guided missile cruiser sails past the western shore of Treasure Island on review in the mid-1980s. (Courtesy of Todd Lappin collection.)

Shown here in the mid-1980s is Naval Station Treasure Island's fire station No. 1, located in Building 157 on the island. Although the naval station is gone, the fire station still remains, now known as San Francisco Fire Station 48. Show are the firefighting apparatus used by the U.S. Navy, including a fire engine in the center, a fire truck at right, and two fire support vehicles at left. The firefighting vehicles have changed, but at the time of publication, the navy fire engine in the center could still be seen in a back lot of the station. (Courtesy of the Todd Lappin collection.)

In addition to a fire department, Naval Station Treasure Island also housed a police station, shown in Building 107. Being a military base, Naval Station Treasure Island wasn't actively patrolled by the San Francisco Police but by military police and a detachment of U.S. Marines. The base also housed a military brig on the northeast corner of the island. The San Francisco Police now patrol Treasure Island from a station located in the main administration building. (Courtesy of the Todd Lappin collection.)

Sailors are pictured at presentation in the reception area of the main administration building on Treasure Island in the mid-1980s. The base chapel can be seen to the rear. The service men and women are looking directly toward downtown San Francisco. (Courtesy of Todd Lappin collection.)

This photograph is a striking image of an otherwise ordinary event. Pictured in the Naval Station Treasure Island PX, a sailor does his shopping while his daughter looks on. She wears his cap. She lives the life of a child growing up on a bustling naval station. One must wonder who was this sailor, how long did he serve on Treasure Island, where is his daughter now, and what memories does she keep of her time on the island? (Courtesy of Todd Lappin collection.)

ACROSS AMERICA, PEOPLE ARE DISCOVERING SOMETHING WONDERFUL. THEIR HERITAGE.

Arcadia Publishing is the leading local history publisher in the United States. With more than 3,000 titles in print and hundreds of new titles released every year, Arcadia has extensive specialized experience chronicling the history of communities and celebrating America's hidden stories, bringing to life the people, places, and events from the past. To discover the history of other communities across the nation, please visit:

www.arcadiapublishing.com

Customized search tools allow you to find regional history books about the town where you grew up, the cities where your friends and family live, the town where your parents met, or even that retirement spot you've been dreaming about.